Traverse Theatre Company

The Nest

by Alan Wilkins

Cast in order of appearance

Colin	Matthew Pidgeon
Helen	Candida Benson
Mac	Lewis Howden
Jackie	Clare Yuille
Innes	Finlay Welsh

Director	Lorne Campbell
Designer	Andrew Burt
Lighting Designer	Maria Bechaalani
Sound Designer	John Harris
Stage Manager	Lee Davis
Deputy Stage Manager	Gemma Smith

**First performed at the Traverse Theatre
Friday 16 April 2004**

TRAVERSE THEATRE

powerhouse of new writing DAILY TELEGRAPH

Artistic Director Philip Howard

The Traverse is Scotland's new writing theatre. Founded in 1963 by a group of maverick artists and enthusiasts, it began as an imaginative attempt to capture the spirit of adventure and experimentation of the Edinburgh Festival all year round. Throughout the decades, the Traverse has evolved and grown in artistic output and ambition. It has refined its mission by strengthening its commitment to producing new plays by Scottish and international playwrights and actively nurturing them throughout their careers. Traverse productions have been seen worldwide and tour regularly throughout the UK and overseas.

The Traverse has produced over 600 new plays in its lifetime and, through a spirit of innovation and risk-taking, has launched the careers of many of the country's best known writers. From, among others, Stanley Eveling in the 1960s, John Byrne in the 1970s, Liz Lochhead in the 1980s, to David Greig and David Harrower in the 1990s, the Traverse is unique in Scotland in its dedication to new writing. It fulfils the crucial role of providing the infrastructure, professional support and expertise to ensure the development of a dynamic theatre culture for Scotland.

The Traverse's activities encompass every aspect of playwriting and pro-duction, providing and facilitating play reading panels, script development workshops, rehearsed readings, public playwriting workshops, writers' groups, a public playwrights' platform, discussions and special events. The Traverse's work with young people is of supreme importance and takes the form of encouraging playwriting through its flagship education project, *Class Act*, as well as the Traverse Young Writers' Group.

Edinburgh's Traverse Theatre is a mini-festival in itself THE TIMES

From its conception in the 1960s, the Traverse has remained a pivotal venue during the Edinburgh Festival. It receives enormous critical and audience acclaim for its programming, as well as regularly winning awards. In 2001 the Traverse was awarded two Scotsman Fringe Firsts and two Herald Angels for its own productions of *Gagarin Way* and *Wiping My Mother's Arse* and a Herald Archangel for overall artistic excellence. Again in 2002 the Traverse produced two award-winning shows, *Outlying Islands* by David Greig and *Iron* by Rona Munro, which both transferred to the Royal Court Theatre, London. In 2003, *The People Next Door* by Henry Adam picked up Fringe First and Herald Angel awards and transferred immediately to the Theatre Royal, Stratford East. Re-cast and with a new director, *The People Next Door* is going out on an international tour in May 2004. Raising its international profile, the Traverse will also develop projects in Japan, China, Portugal and France in 2004.

For further information on the Traverse Theatre's activities and history, an online resource is available at www.virtualtraverse.co.uk. To find out about ways to support the Traverse, please contact Norman MacLeod, Development Manager on 0131 228 3223.

www.traverse.co.uk • www.virtualtraverse.co.uk

ALAN WILKINS

On certain spring days in Edinburgh frequent gusts of a fiercely cutting
wind remind us that there is another country out there, very distant from
the elegant certainties of the New Town, and very different from the civic
patina overlaid on the city by the multi-coloured crocuses peeping through
manicured park lawns. That country is the more rugged Scotland, the
Scotland of bare, storm-swept mountains and seemingly endless rain-
drenched moors.

Those places may be ones which the majority have never seen and to which
most will never go, but we know that they are there and that mentally, if
not physically, they surround us. We harbour a curious, ill-informed pride
about them and we think we would like to explore them, if only vicariously
– hence the enthusiasm for stories of mountaineering endeavour and
brushes with high-altitude death. They speak to us of drama, and of a life
where dangerous events can be – and are – played out free of domestic
restraints and with a raw intensity we often feel we lack.

Of course some people do go there and some even develop obsessions
about it. Chief amongst these is collecting – the sporting term for it is
'bagging' – Munros and its manifestation is the driving desire to stand at
the summit of each one of the 284 peaks in Scotland which are more than
3000 feet tall.

Alan Wilkins has that desire, but not obsessively so. He has 'bagged' only
just under sixty and when the opportunity arises to add to the list he is just
as likely to do other, perhaps more challenging, things.

Last summer he walked from Montrose to Morar, right across Scotland.
Motivated by a curiosity about his country – a curiosity that often arises
within those who have spent time living elsewhere (in his case Poland and
Spain) – he also took the opportunity to visit as many bothies as he could
in order to find the one that most exactly matched his mental image of the
setting for his new play set amongst the Munros – *The Nest*.

The enclosed space that is the crucible for the action of *The Nest* is not an
exact replica of the bothy near Sgurr Mor, but it is very similar. Both have
an open fire and both are sited in wild country. The living space in both is
also accessible only from below, through a trap door. Like being born into
a new world, no one can come onto set in this play elegantly or without a
struggle. And that is like going into the mountains too.

The Nest is Alan Wilkins' third play, but the first to receive a professional
production. His earliest – *Childish Things* – he himself describes as being
'a typical start-out'. Its follow-up, set in Madrid, is still in his drawer
waiting for a production. Both however achieved performed readings and
it was these readings that encouraged the Traverse to commission the
work which, two years in the writing, is now launching a new career for
him as a full-time dramatist.

Brought up in Edinburgh, Alan cut his theatrical teeth – like David Greig,
another Traverse-commissioned writer – with Edinburgh Youth Theatre.
After a degree in English Literature at Glasgow University, he earned a
living as an actor for a couple of years, and although he enjoyed the
challenges, including time spent with Suspect Culture and Borderline –
and the inevitable non-speaking part in *Take the High Road* – he

increasingly began to think of a different future. Taking a TEFL course he worked abroad but more re-assessment led to teacher training and six years in the drama department of Inverkeithing High School.

His approach to promoting his plays was disarmingly simple. Knowing the constant reputation of the Traverse for encouraging new Scottish writing, he simply sent *Childish Things* to the theatre and got an encouraging response. But his approach to the future after *The Nest* has been more determined: a fire in his tenement block late last year from which he had to be rescued and after which he was hospitalised made him think, in his own words, 'What the hell?'. Hence the decision to focus on writing full-time.

On the evidence of *The Nest* the prospects for this 34-year-old are likely to be bright. Admittedly the device of placing five people together in enforced isolation and seeing what happens is conventional enough – the stuff of many detective stories and even more films. So perhaps is the story of one of the couples, who, at a moment that is meant to be of shared success (more Munro-bagging) are heading instead for the failure of separation. But the surrounding characters provide a more unusual counterpoint – a young photographer who has the faults and virtues of hedonistic youth, a bodyguard to the rich and famous who has a problem with honesty as well as image and an old man carrying something unexpected and horrific.

In these terms *The Nest* is not so much about the exterior that is all around us, but about the interior that we carry within us. It is also about those unsung and often un-remembered individuals who are, in whatever terms, unusual and even heroic and who can inspire others to actions that they would normally not even consider. Surprisingly for such a modern play, one of the background stories that Alan has drawn on is that of the 'Buchanites', a strange, Ayrshire-based, 18th-century sect whose leader, one Elspeth Buchan, instructed her followers to wait for her return after death. One did, for all of his life.

The Nest might have been an opportunity for indulging in the Gothic – the terrors of isolation unleashing forces beyond our control. Although at the beginning it cleverly toys with the audience along those lines, the play actually confronts the much more interesting issue of who we are and how we interact in a world in which success in understanding human relationships and our own problems and possibilities are the most difficult matters of all. This is not a particularly Scottish issue – it is universal – but the setting and the nuances make this is a particularly Scottish play as does the celebration of the wilds of Scotland and of her culture, a love of which are clearly deeply embedded in the playwright.

Alan Wilkins is at the start of his writing career. It may be, as most are, strewn with pitfalls and periods when having other strings to his bow are essential. But *The Nest* indicates that his lively interest in what (and who) is around him is a prime motivator and that is usually the best indication of a talent that can survive. *The Nest* is an enquiring play, rather than one which simply answers all the questions: a play, in other words, that is about the real world – a world as real, exciting and potentially threatening as the mountains in which it is set.

Michael Russell
Writer and commentator, Argyll, March 2004

Alan Wilkins was brought up in Edinburgh and, after time spent in Glasgow, Poznan and Madrid, returned there in 1998. After graduating from Glasgow University he worked as an actor before working as a TEFL teacher for three years abroad. On returning to the UK, he then qualified and worked as a teacher of Drama. His first play, CHILDISH THINGS, was given a rehearsed reading at the Traverse in June 1998. His second, CAFETERIA / RESTAURANT, was produced as part of a series of rehearsed readings at the Tron for the Scottish-Italian festival in October 1999. THE NEST is Alan's third play and his first to receive a professional production.

COMPANY BIOGRAPHIES

Maria Bechaalani (Lighting Designer) Trained: Bristol Old Vic Theatre School. For the Traverse: THE BALLAD OF CRAZY PAOLA, HIGHLAND SHORTS. Other theatre includes: INNIT . . . INNAT, MAINTAIN (Freshmess); 1000 AEROPLANES, ON THE ROOF, VOICEOVER (Paragon Ensemble); BRAZIL (Theatre of Imagination); ROMEO & JULIET, WHILE THE SUN SHINES, THE SLAB BOYS (Byre); REMEMBERING HILDEGARDE (Lung Ha's).

Candida Benson (Helen) Trained: RADA. For the Traverse: SLEEP OF THE JUST. Other theatre includes: NOTHING, PRIVATE LIVES, THE FOUR TWINS, THE NUN, CAVALCADE, RAMEAU'S NEPHEW (Citizens); BLACKBIRD (Southwark Playhouse); PICASSO'S WOMEN (National, Cottesloe). Television work includes: MIDSOMER MURDERS (Bentley); KAVANAGH QC (Carlton); PROMETHEUS (Channel 4). Film includes: NICHOLAS NICKLEBY (Nickleby Films); HOMESICK (Halo Productions); EYELINES (Diverse Productions).

Andrew Burt (Designer) Trained: Glasgow University and Central St. Martin's College, London. Design credits include: THE CARETAKER (Citizens); THE PHILEDELPHIA STORY, BRUTOPIA, HAYFEVER (RSAMD); TERRI MCINTYRE, FRANS PEOPLE (BBC Scotland); THE BOOK ROOM, DEADPAN (The Arches).

Lorne Campbell (Director) Trained: RSAMD and Liverpool John Moores. Lorne joined the Traverse in 2002 on the Channel 4 Theatre Director's Scheme. During this time he has been Assistant Director on DARK EARTH, OUTLYING ISLANDS, MR PLACEBO, HOMERS and THE SLAB BOYS TRILOGY. THE NEST is Lorne's first production for the Traverse. Before joining the Traverse, Lorne ran Forge Theatre Company. His directing credits include: DEATH AND THE MAIDEN, THE CHEVIOT, THE STAG AND THE BLACK BLACK OIL, THE CHAIRS, THE DUMB WAITER, COMEDY OF ERRORS, OLEANNA.

John Harris (Sound Designer) For the Traverse: KNIVES IN HENS, ANNA WEISS, PERFECT DAYS, FAMILY, GRETA, SHARP SHORTS.

Other theatre includes: DRUMMERS (out of joint); LAND OF CAKES (Dundee Rep); URFAUST (RSAMD); IL BELLISSIMO SILENCIO, OF NETTLES AND ROSES, STOCKAREE (Theatre Workshop, Edinburgh). Film / animation includes: THE EMPEROR (C4); THE GREEN MAN OF KNOWLEDGE (S4C). Film includes: PATER NOSTER (eight and a half); BEACHES (Red Kite). John has been Artistic Director of the Paragon Ensemble since 2001.

Lewis Howden (Mac) For the Traverse: OLGA, KNIVES IN HENS, LOOSE ENDS, THE HOUSE AMONG THE STARS. Other theatre includes NIGHTINGALE AND CHASE (Citizens); BEAUTY QUEEN OF LEENANNE, THE TRICK IS TO KEEP BREATHING (Tron); MOTHER COURAGE, CUTTIN' A RUG, MERLIN THE MAGNIFICENT (Royal Lyceum, Edinburgh); THE CRUCIBLE, GLENGARRY GLEN ROSS, THE BIG FUNK (The Arches); MEDEA, KING LEAR, MACBETH (Theatre Babel); FIRE IN THE BASEMENT (Communicado). Television work includes: TURNING WORLD (Channel 4); MONARCH OF THE GLEN, STRATHBLAIR (BBC); TAGGART, REBUS, DR FINLAY (STV). Film includes: ABERDEEN (Freeway Films); THE BLUE BOY (BBC); GARE AU MALE (Animula).

Matthew Pidgeon (Colin) Trained: RSAMD. Theatre includes: 8000m (Suspect Culture); THE LYING KIND (Royal Court); BRIGHTON BEACH MEMOIRS, OTHELLO (Byre); ANTIGONE, THE PHOENIX, THE GRAPES OF WRATH (7:84); CAUCASIAN CHALK CIRCLE, HAMLET, MONTROSE, THE GLASS MENAGERIE, ROMEO & JULIET (Royal Lyceum, Edinburgh). Television work includes: THIS MORNING WITH RICHARD NOT JUDY, CASUALTY (BBC); TAGGART (STV); PSYCHOS (Channel 4). Film includes: THE WINSLOW BOY (Winslow Partners Ltd); A SHOT AT GLORY (Butcher's Run Films); STATE & MAIN (Filmtown Entertainment).

Finlay Welsh (Innes) For the Traverse: FAITH HEALER, SHINING SOULS, AWAY, BROTHERS OF THUNDER, EUROPE, STREET FIGHTING MAN, SOMERVILLE THE SOLDIER, THE DEAD OF NIGHT, GYNT!. Other theatre includes: GAGARIN WAY (Prime Cuts, Belfast); THE ENTERTAINER (Citizens); TRANSLATIONS, MUCH ADO ABOUT NOTHING, THE TAMING OF THE SHREW, THE ANATOMIST (Royal Lyceum, Edinburgh); MEDEA, ELECTRA, OEDIPUS, TWELFTH NIGHT (Theatre Babel). Television work includes: TAGGART (STV); THE PRACTICALITY OF MAGNOLIA (Hopscotch Films); STILL GAME (BBC). Film includes: BREAKING THE WAVES (Argus Film Produktie); TRAINSPOTTING (Channel Four Films); BEING HUMAN (BSB).

Clare Yuille (Jackie) Trained: RSAMD. Theatre includes: SAUCHIEHALL STREET (Vanishing Point); THE PRINCESS AND THE GOBLIN, THE PRIME OF MISS JEAN BRODIE (Royal Lyceum, Edinburgh). Television work includes: RIVER CITY (BBC Talent); FLASHES (Winding Road Film Productions). Radio work includes: TUESDAYS AND SUNDAYS, THE CHRONYCLE (BBC RADIO 4).

SPONSORSHIP

Sponsorship income enables the Traverse to commission
and produce new plays and to offer audiences a diverse and
exciting programme of events throughout the year

We would like to thank the following companies
for their support throughout the year

CORPORATE SPONSORS

 BBC Scotland  smg tv productions  KPMG

 (UK) LIMITED
www.acseurope.com

LAURENCE SMITH & SON
(EDINBURGH) LTD
WINE AND SPIRIT SHIPPERS
Established 1883

 BAIRDS fine and country wines

Canon  ARCAS Computing Ltd. pinnacle communications ltd

 STEWARTS

NICHOLAS
GROVES
RAINES
ARCHITECTS

CHAMPAGNE
ALAIN THIENOT
REIMS · FRANCE

 Wired Nomad

ANNIVERSARY ANGELS

 bu edi
A Burrell Company/EDI Group Joint Venture

edNET
internetworkingsolutions

 BENNETT & ROBERTSON LLP

 Priority Management Training
People & Projects

 Jean McGhee
RECRUITMENT

 Whiteburn
projects limited

 BAILLIE GIFFORD

 New Horizons
Computer Learning Centers
Scotland

This theatre has the support of the Pearson Playwright's Scheme sponsored by Pearson plc

With thanks to

Douglas Hall of IMPact Human Resourcing for management advice arranged through the Arts & Business skills bank. Claire Aitken of Royal Bank of Scotland for mentoring support arranged through the Arts & Business Mentoring Scheme. Purchase of the Traverse Box Office, computer network and technical and training equipment has been made possible with money from The Scottish Arts Council National Lottery Fund

Scottish
Arts Council
LOTTERY FUNDED

**The Traverse Theatre's work
would not be possible without the support of**

Scottish
Arts Council

·EDINBVRGH·
THE CITY OF EDINBURGH COUNCIL

The Traverse Theatre receives financial assistance from

The Calouste Gulbenkian Foundation, The Peggy Ramsay Foundation, The Binks Trust, The Bulldog Prinsep Theatrical Fund, The Esmée Fairbairn Foundation, The Gordon Fraser Charitable Trust, The Garfield Weston Foundation, The Paul Hamlyn Foundation, The Craignish Trust, Lindsay's Charitable Trust, The Tay Charitable Trust, The Ernest Cook Trust, The Wellcome Trust, The Sir John Fisher Foundation, The Ruben and Elisabeth Rausing Trust, The Equity Trust Fund, The Cross Trust, N Smith Charitable Settlement, Douglas Heath Eves Charitable Trust, The Bill and Margaret Nicol Charitable Trust, The Emile Littler Foundation, Mrs M Guido's Charitable Trust, Gouvernement du Québec, The Canadian High Commission, The British Council

Charity No. SC002368

Sets, props and costumes for
The Nest

created by Traverse Workshops
(funded by the National Lottery)

 Scottish
Arts Council
LOTTERY FUNDED

Production photography by Douglas Robertson

Print photography by Euan Myles

**For their continued generous support
of Traverse productions the Traverse thanks**

Habitat

Marks and Spencer, Princes Street

Camerabase

BHS

**For their support on
The Nest,
Alan Wilkins would like to thank**

Ardroy Outdoor Education Centre, Argyll
Argus Hotel, Edinburgh
Casino Café, Cadaques
Cove Park, Peaton Hill, Cove, Helensburgh

TRAVERSE THEATRE – THE COMPANY

THE NEST

Alan Wilkins

For Emily
who will be walking soon

Characters

COLIN, *in his late thirties. Formerly an art lecturer, now works in a garden centre.*

HELEN, *in her thirties. Works in a Further Education College. Married to Colin for twelve years.*

INNES, *seventy years old, or thereabouts. A self-made man.*

JACKIE, *in her twenties. A photographer.*

MAC, *in his early forties. A bodyguard.*

The action takes place in a bothy, close to the mountain of Sgurr Mor in Scotland.

PART ONE

8.00 in the evening.

The action takes place in a bothy in the Western Highland area of Scotland.

The stage is fairly bare, as befits a bothy. Downstage centre is an open trap door. All characters climb up a ladder to appear from this when they enter, or descend it to exit. There are no other entrances or exits. Centre-stage right is a fireplace, with a pile of logs and kindling beside it. Stage left of the fireplace is a low table; three plastic school chairs are stacked against the back wall. Some books, including old visitors' books, are on the mantelpiece above the fire. Another shelf on the same wall has some salt, some candles in bottles, a tin of rice pudding and some Gore-tex boot spray. Some old walking/outdoor magazines are on the table. The windows are slanted into the shape of the roof.

The area below – the ground floor of the bothy – is never seen. Some articles of bothy maintenance e.g. a ladder, logs would be stored there. There may also be mice.

The catch on the front door is heard and the sound of a pack being dumped.

COLIN (*offstage, below*). I'll go up.

HELEN. No, I'll go. (*Sound of* HELEN *ascending the ladder. She appears onstage. It is impossible to do this elegantly. She stands up and looks around.*) It's empty.

COLIN *climbs up. Her rucksack appears first. She takes it and waits for* COLIN's *to appear. When it does, she dumps both of them in the main space of the bothy and sits down in an armchair.* COLIN *pulls himself up.*

COLIN (*looks around*). There's a rucksack.

HELEN. Empty of people, I meant. Not objects.

COLIN. We were going to pitch the tent . . .

HELEN. You were. Inside dry, outside wet. I'm staying here. Besides, people leave bags in bothies. Pop up a hill, pick it up later and carry on walking. We might still have the place to ourselves.

COLIN. They'd have left it downstairs. And there's a carrymat out. They've staked a sleeping space.

HELEN. So we've got company. It's a good bothy. There might be a crowd by the end of the day. What's the problem?

COLIN. Well I . . . I carried the tent. If we'd talked about this earlier, I'd have left it at home. But I carried it.

HELEN. Yes.

She unhooks her carrymat and sets out her space – e.g. sleeping bag and a makeshift pillow against the wall. COLIN *does the same.* HELEN *lights a cigarette.*

COLIN. I thought you didn't smoke in bothies.

HELEN. There's no-one else here. And I'm not climbing down that ladder just for a cigarette.

COLIN. It's all wood in here.

HELEN. I'll be careful.

COLIN. Could go up like that.

HELEN. Yes. You're right. Vigilance will be necessary.

COLIN. If it's left smouldering . . .

HELEN. We'll die in our expensive down sleeping bags.

COLIN. And so will they. (*Pointing at the other sleeping space.*)

HELEN. That's not down. (HELEN *now starts to set up a Primus stove to boil up some water.*)

COLIN. That couple we saw from the col. They looked like they were heading here.

HELEN. Very possibly.

COLIN. Though they'd probably be here by now. We might get away with it.

HELEN. It's a bothy. You can't be precious about it. We might end up sharing with twenty German scouts again.

COLIN. That was a good night.

HELEN. Exactly.

COLIN. But for this trip – well, I suppose it's tomorrow night that matters. It'd be good to be alone then. Shall we pitch the tent tomorrow?

HELEN. Let's decide that then.

COLIN (*looks around*). The place is in good nick. Rubbish in the fireplace – that's lazy.

HELEN (*automatically – as if imitating*). If you can carry it in, you can carry it out.

COLIN. It's not a lot to ask. Still, we'll want a fire later. Most of it will burn.

HELEN. And we can carry the crushed tins out. Do our bit.

COLIN. Apart from that, it's good. Clean. Is that hot enough yet?

HELEN. No.

COLIN. It's not the quickest. We should upgrade. That is . . . if . . . Helen, I would like this to carry on. After tomorrow.

HELEN *says nothing – by now she is back in an armchair looking at the cover of an outdoor magazine.*

Helen . . .

HELEN. What?

COLIN. I said I would like this to carry on. After tomorrow. I would like to upgrade our stove. I'd like there to be some point to that.

HELEN. Let's talk about it after.

COLIN. There's tons we could do. Corbetts, Grahams, trail-walking . . . trekking overseas – the Atlas mountains.

HELEN. They won't let you take stoves on planes anymore.

COLIN. I think that's just the canisters.

HELEN. Colin . . . we need to talk about what happens next. You're right. But not now. Tomorrow. Or the next day. No . . . tomorrow.

COLIN. It's just . . . you seem . . . not to be enjoying this.

HELEN (*looking around*). What's not to enjoy?

COLIN (*looks at her, uncertain as to whether to continue*).
Only, I've had an idea. About tomorrow. (HELEN *pours
tea,* COLIN *produces an Ordnance Survey map, sits down
next to her and unfolds it over the table.*) Here we are, right.
(*Despite herself,* HELEN *loves a map.*)

HELEN. Yes.

COLIN. Tomorrow, we leave the heavy stuff here, retrace our
steps – crossing the river at the same spot as today. Follow
the path west, until it turns north-east. Over Sgurr Beag and
then the final pull, up to Sgurr Mor. The weather is perfect;
clear, some sun. We open champagne, toast each other and –
probably – though I can't guarantee it – a golden eagle rises
from below us and soars majestically high above us.

HELEN (*sadly*). It sounds good.

COLIN. We kiss. (*Silence.*) We agree. The game can't end
here. We descend back the way we came but leave the path
here, skirting round the 300m contour. We trudge up – a
head-on, steep slog of an ascent until we reach the summit
of Fraoch Bheinn. Only now it's in cloud. There's no view.
No eagles. It starts to rain. We decide on a direct easterly
descent, but it's tricky at times. It's been a long day and by
the time we've reached the easy stuff, we're exhausted. The
last bit of descent takes forever, bits of path appear and
disappear until finally – we're back here. The last Munro
and the first Corbett. (*Silence.*) I know we've done a few
already, but the first Corbett of Us Doing The Corbetts.
What do you think?

HELEN. Fraoch Bheinn's the middle of three. It's madness to
pick it off as a singleton. We should either have a longer
day and head south-west from the path to take in Sgurr
Cos-na . . . No. That's not the point. I'm not ready for a new
plan. The old one's not done yet.

Sound of the door opening below.

MAC (*from below*). Hullo. Anybody in?

HELEN. Upstairs.

MAC (*his head appearing through the trap door*). Is that a brew?

COLIN. It's almost ready.

MAC. There's two of us.

COLIN (*doubtfully*). There might be enough.

MAC (*quieter*). Just pour one then. (HELEN *pours.*) Thanks. Anybody else in?

HELEN. One other sleeping bag.

MAC (*to below*). Plenty of room, hen.

JACKIE (*from below*). Don't call me hen.

MAC (*drinks tea*). God, I needed this.

HELEN. Are you coming up?

MAC. Aye. Why not? (*Hauls himself up.*) Lovely. (*Lies down, his head disappearing into the hatch, but still audible.*) Just lift it a bit, so I can reach . . . it's not that heavy.

JACKIE (*from below*). It fucking is.

MAC. Try.

JACKIE. I am fucking trying.

MAC. You're almost there. Come on. Got it. (MAC *pulls an enormous rucksack that just fits through the hole. He heaves it to one side then resumes his previous position.*) Now yours. (*He pulls up a polythene bag, with a tripod sticking out of it, then a daysack. He turns to* COLIN *and* HELEN.) Hi.

JACKIE (*from below*). What about me?

MAC. Sorry. (*Resumes his position and helps* JACKIE *through.*)

JACKIE. Hi. Is that tea?

COLIN. It's finished. Sorry.

MAC (*offers his*). A bit left. Finish it.

JACKIE (*looks around*). Is this it?

MAC. This is a good one.

COLIN. Very clean.

JACKIE. You said it was a house.

MAC. I said it was a bothy. You didn't know what a bothy was, so I said it was like a house. And it is. Kind of.

HELEN. If you dragged her up here by saying there'd be anything 'like a house' at the end, you owe her a huge apology.

MAC. I didn't drag her up anything. There's rubbish in the fireplace. I hate that.

COLIN. I know.

MAC. If you can carry it in, you can carry it out. (MAC *makes the fire for the next few minutes.*)

JACKIE. He's right. He didn't drag me anywhere. I only met him an hour ago. I'm Jackie by the way.

HELEN. Helen.

COLIN. I'm Colin.

JACKIE. You smoke? Do you want one?

HELEN. Sure. Thanks.

MAC. Bit dodgy in a bothy. (COLIN *nods.*)

JACKIE. You're building a fire.

MAC. My favourite bothy burnt down. Nothing left of it. One cigarette, one whisky too many and that was it. The Nest was gone.

JACKIE. You said this was the Nest.

MAC. When the Nest went, this became my favourite bothy. But I can't say its name. So I call it the Nest.

JACKIE. What's its real name?

MAC. Kil-something.

COLIN. Kinbreack.

JACKIE. That's not difficult.

MAC. Just always comes out wrong. The Nest is easier.

JACKIE. I'll be careful. With the cigarette.

MAC. Give us a draw. (JACKIE *does so.*) That's good. (*Hands it back.*)

JACKIE (*to* COLIN). Where are we?

COLIN (*adjusts map and points out the bothy*). Just here. Where did you start from?

JACKIE. Invergarry. I got a lift to the dam and started walking, just looking for somewhere to set up the camera. Only, I stopped for a break at a waterfall and when I started again, there seemed to be two paths. I wasn't sure which one to take. Then it started raining. I looked at the time and realised I had to turn back. So I did, but actually I was carrying on. Until this lunatic came running down the hill. He brought me here.

MAC. Lunatic's harsh.

JACKIE. Running. With a pack that size.

MAC. It was getting dark. It is dark now. We just made it.

JACKIE. And I'm grateful. You're not a lunatic. Thanks.

MAC. Being in Glen Kingie without a map or compass. That's lunacy.

HELEN. You've no map or compass?

JACKIE. I've had my row, thanks. I'll never do it again, I think I can promise that.

HELEN. You're very lucky.

JACKIE. I know. I could have been sleeping rough for the night.

HELEN. No. You could've died. (*Silence.*)

JACKIE. Possibly . . .

COLIN. Well . . .

JACKIE. Shit . . . Have you saved my life?

MAC. We'll never know. But don't get all serious. I preferred it when you just thought I'd done you a favour. Feel free to keep calling me a stupid arse.

JACKIE. You did lead me into a bog that went up to my knees . . . Christ . . . thank you.

MAC. Last time I want to hear it.

HELEN. We'll walk you back tomorrow.

COLIN. Helen!

HELEN. This is more important.

MAC. Don't worry, we've got it covered. (MAC *has lit the fire*.) I'm heading east tomorrow for Meall na Teanga. I can drop on to the Glen Dessary road from here. It's not a problem. Easier in fact.

COLIN. Quite a trek to do it over the hills.

MAC. Sometimes that thing feels as light as a handbag – you're in a groove and can walk for miles. Other days . . . I hate it. I hate every ounce of it. The last thing you want on a day like that is a peat bog. A day on the road . . . well, it could be worse.

HELEN. How long have you carried that for?

MAC. Two months now.

COLIN. A continuous?

MAC. Hopefully. Over halfway now, with Knoydart taken care of, but there's some real bastards left.

JACKIE. A continuous? A continuous what?

HELEN. A continuous walk over all the Munros. Scottish mountains over three thousand feet.

JACKIE. I'm not sure I understand.

HELEN. You know that hill you were on?

JACKIE. Yes.

HELEN. That's one. There's two hundred and eighty-four of them. Some people try and climb them all. Some try and climb them all in one go.

COLIN (*to* MAC). Transport?

MAC. No . . . Except Mull, of course.

COLIN. I'd love to do something like that.

MAC (*looks at him doubtfully*). Maybe you could . . .

COLIN. Let's just say . . . that after today, I'll need a new challenge. (*Pause.*)

HELEN. He's completing.

MAC. Brilliant mate. Well done.

JACKIE. He's finishing the thing you're doing.

HELEN. Yes . . . it just took him a bit longer, that's all.

COLIN. Five years . . . But it's not just . . .

JACKIE. Look, I'm not being rude, but has anyone got any food? That they don't need, of course.

HELEN. We've got our emergency rations.

JACKIE. Emergency rations? God, you take this seriously, don't you?

HELEN. Well, we take food up mountains, yes.

COLIN. And we do kind of need it. In case there's an emergency.

HELEN. A woman in a bothy with no food – that is an emergency.

JACKIE. No, I'll manage.

MAC. I've a tin of fruit spare. And we'll have to have a drink later – to celebrate with you.

COLIN. Like I said, it's not just me.

MAC. What's the last one? No, let me guess . . . Gairich?

HELEN. Sgurr Mor.

COLIN. Helen's finishing as well. We did them together.

MAC (*as he goes for his rucksack*). It's a hell of an achievement. Let's have that drink now.

HELEN. It's been a hobby. You can't toast a hobby. It's nothing really.

JACKIE. A drink's a drink. Good call. (MAC *uses the two flask mugs and a couple of old cups from the bothy shelf.*)

MAC. I'd advise a bit of water. It's cask-proof – strong stuff. (*This is too late for* COLIN, *who splutters.*)

COLIN. Jesus.

MAC. Rock star I used to work for. I got him out of a tricky situation once. He gave me life membership of the Malt Whisky Society, as a thank-you. That's class.

JACKIE. Look – say no if you want, but . . . can I take your photograph?

COLIN. Of course.

HELEN (*at the same time*). No thanks.

Silence.

JACKIE. Just a snap. I'm not going to get the tripod and deck the place up like a studio. Just a snap with the digital. I'll e-mail it to you.

HELEN. There's no need.

JACKIE. It's what I do. It'll be a good picture. I've had a shit day because I took a shit commission and I don't know where to look for ptarmigans or crossbills. But this . . . capturing a moment, this is bread and butter.

HELEN (*giving in – a slight moment of relaxation*). OK.

JACKIE, *instantly, takes a photo.*

COLIN. I wasn't ready.

HELEN. Professionals take their time. (MAC *laughs.*)

JACKIE. Trust me. It'll work. That was the second – a moment later would have been no good. This'll have the togetherness, but the tension as well. (*Silence.*)

COLIN (*quietly*). A bit honest, Jackie. For a bothy.

JACKIE. They seem like honest places. I'd still rather be in a house, mind you.

MAC. Whose is the bag?

HELEN. We don't know.

MAC. It's getting late.

JACKIE. It's 8.20.

MAC. If it's dark, it's late. Weather's not so good either. (*Goes to rucksack, takes out a pair of night-vision binoculars.*)

HELEN. Night-vision binoculars? I'm not surprised that's heavy.

MAC. I like my toys. I'm going up a hundred metres. Just to scan. That bag's beginning to concern me.

COLIN (*nods*). I'll come with you.

JACKIE. Boys to the rescue.

MAC (*to* COLIN). No, you stay here. Jackie, bring your camera.

JACKIE. I'm not leaving.

MAC. It'll be worth it. A late-dusk light – dark, brooding mountain shapes, a moon, a desirable male model. Trust me.

JACKIE (*sensing an agenda*). OK.

JACKIE grabs her jacket and begins the descent. MAC quickly behind her. From below:

Ah ma hand, you big bastard.

MAC. Sorry. (*Waits then lowers himself down. When his head only is visible above the floor, he looks at* COLIN *and* HELEN.) Look . . . (*Exits.*)

Silence.

COLIN. They left because of us. (*Another silence.* HELEN *goes for her whisky, takes a sip.*) Look, I know people get depressed. After they've finished. But we're doing them together. We'll face afterwards together. We've climbed two hundred and eighty-three of the Munros. We've got one more to go. I wanted just to be with you tonight but we chose the bothy and . . . they seem all right. Why don't we celebrate together? All four – or five of us.

Silence.

HELEN. Do you remember why we started?

COLIN. Yes. To do something together.

HELEN. And whose idea was it?

COLIN. Yours, I think . . . I don't know, we had lots of ideas.

HELEN. I remember . . . bee-keeping, joining a choir – they all went into the hat. The desperate search for something to do together because being together wasn't enough – wasn't bearable. So who suggested the doing? Who got paid to tell us we should get a hobby?

COLIN. Sheena, her name was. I think.

HELEN. That's right. You betrayed me and Sheena, the marriage guidance counsellor, told us to get a hobby.

COLIN. She wasn't telling us to run away from the problem. She was telling us to . . . avoid problems. She was telling us to talk.

HELEN. We don't talk. We walk. We break the silence sometimes to talk about walking. And when we do, we talk about the best bits of the day – a scramble, a head-down, hard-breathing trudge, a battle against the wind on a ridge – they're all bits we did on our own. Silently. (*Pause.*) I always thought a hobby was just . . . too easy in the penance department. (*Gets up and moves to the mantelpiece and looks through old A4 notebooks.*) I'm sorry, Colin. I really am. You hurt me so much more than you thought, so much more than a hobby could fix, but I'm sorry.

COLIN. Don't be. I had no idea. I thought . . . I thought we'd moved on. If this has brought it back, I'm sorry. You're right. I did get off lightly.

HELEN. Read this.

COLIN (*takes one of the A4 notebooks from her, open at the right page*). The Visitors' Book.

HELEN. The bottom of the page.

COLIN (*reading*). 'Climbed Sgurr Mor, my first Munro. Many thanks to Fran for help in planning. At the top, under a stone, I buried a photograph of my husband. Helen, Galashiels.' Christ. (*Silence.*)

HELEN. I thought we were happily married. I was wrong. You thought we'd made it up. You were wrong. We're . . . maybe we're quits.

COLIN. I had one affair.

HELEN. One more than was right.

COLIN. You've . . . you've already finished them.

HELEN. I was always one ahead. We were never doing them together.

COLIN. But . . . I don't understand.

HELEN. Neither did I.

COLIN. We worked it out.

HELEN. I thought we had something special. Then I found out I was wrong. I wanted you to know how that felt.

Silence. HELEN *sips whisky, plays with a cigarette.*

COLIN. Moving to Galashiels. That was your idea. Away from the city, away from temptation. It took me one second to decide. I changed job – your idea. I didn't just take up a hobby. I committed myself to you.

HELEN. You'd already done that once. I wasn't sure how much it was worth.

The sound of JACKIE *and* MAC *returning.*

JACKIE *(from below)*. You go first.

MAC *(from below)*. Aye, so you can look at my arse.

JACKIE *(from below)*. Just get up there.

COLIN. Why didn't you just leave me?

HELEN. I think, perhaps, I just have.

MAC *(emerging)*. No sign of him.

HELEN. Of who?

MAC. Missing rucksack man.

HELEN. Man?

MAC. Point taken. Statistical probability though.

JACKIE *(emerging)*. It's hell out there. We didn't look far.

MAC. Is he alright? (COLIN *is gazing at the visitors' book.*)

HELEN. I . . . I don't know.

COLIN. I'm fine. Fine. I just need a bit of fresh air. I'll be back in a while.

MAC. Don't be daft. It's worse than miserable out there.

COLIN. I won't be long. I'll just stand at the door. (COLIN *exits.*)

MAC. You got a phone?

HELEN. Yes.

JACKIE. Yes.

MAC. Have you checked for reception? (*Both check and shake their heads.*)

JACKIE. Fuck. I said I'd phone my flatmate.

MAC. It was always a long shot. No idea where he was walking anyway. Nothing we can do. He'll probably turn up. It's dark now though. He can't have much gear with him, leaving his rucksack like that. Maybe left a route-card or a note in his bag. (*To* HELEN.) You alright?

HELEN. Don't worry about me.

MAC. Will he be alright?

HELEN. Why wouldn't he be?

MAC. I don't know.

HELEN. No, you don't.

MAC. Do you know how heavy my rucksack is?

JACKIE. Too heavy.

MAC. Twenty-seven kilos.

HELEN. Christ.

MAC. Sometimes less, twenty-five or so. Usually twenty-seven. I like gear, I like luxury. This is an unsupported trip. There's no-one burying food parcels for me. But that's not the only reason. In my pack there's a large blue rock. 280 million years old – approximately. Beautiful. Weighs about four kilograms. (*Pause.*) Just though I'd share that with you.

JACKIE. Why?

MAC. I've not told anyone before. I meet people, they see me suffering and they give advice. Lose some of the pack weight, don't bother with gaiters, cut your bloody toothbrush down. And I just grin like an idiot. I've got a beautiful four-kilogram rock in my pack and you want me to pare my toothbrush down. It always makes me laugh. But other times . . . on my own, I just feel stupid. For four days I had a knot of pain at the top of my spine. I had to take a break every twenty minutes. I'd forget why I was doing this.

JACKIE. Why are you doing it?

MAC. At the moment, I've forgotten. I thought it might be a tag – if I wanted to write a book about the trip. 'Round Scotland with a Fucking Big Pack.'

HELEN (*smiling for the first time in a while*). 'The Munros with a Big Blue Rock.'

JACKIE. 'Round Moldova with a Fucking Fridge.' I hate that. Ordinary stuff with an angle. Write an interesting book about an interesting subject – people will read it. Take good, interesting photographs – people will look at them.

MAC. The angle gets the publishers interested. I'm not a purist. I know what you mean but . . . it's a beautiful rock, so I'll keep on carrying it. (*Pause. HELEN takes the visitors' book and puts it back on the mantelpiece. The rain picks up.*) He should come in now.

JACKIE. Can I see the rock?

MAC. I've told you about it. No reason not to show you, I suppose. Except . . . maybe you won't like it. That'd be the last thing I'd need. No. Not yet. We need to get Colin in and work out what to do about rucksack person.

JACKIE. There's nothing we can do.

MAC. Look for a route-card. Always a possibility.

HELEN. You can't go out in that.

MAC. I wouldn't like to find them dead two hundred metres away tomorrow morning. I'll have a look. If there's nothing there, I'll go out and get Colin in. Can you keep the fire going? He's going to be cold and wet. (JACKIE *attends to the fire. MAC goes to the spare carrymat and rucksack and looks for a route-card. None there.*) I'll just open the top section – that's the only place they'd have left one.

HELEN. It would be attached to the outside. You wouldn't leave a route-card inside.

MAC. Probably right. I'm not going to steal anything though. Just have a look. (*Opens rucksack.*) Jesus Christ.

JACKIE. What?

MAC. Fucking hell.

JACKIE. What?

MAC. Fuck.

JACKIE. A big, blue, beautiful rock?

MAC. No. (*Pulls out an old bible.*) There's more.

> MAC *pulls out a skull. Thunder. Noise of rain increases*
> *again. The sound of the door opening as* COLIN *comes in.*

COLIN. Mac . . . give us a hand.

MAC. Coming.

> MAC *lies on his stomach, head down over the trap door,*
> *helping to pull* INNES *up. As he does this,* JACKIE *goes to*
> *the rucksack and looks inside.*

JACKIE. There's more. Probably a whole body.

> JACKIE *quickly takes a photograph of the skull. She lines*
> *up and takes a second, which is the first thing that* INNES
> *sees as he is hauled up through the trap door by* MAC. *He*
> *is old – in his seventies – and soaked through.*

HELEN (*to* INNES.) Are you alright?

INNES. John Anderson my jo, John . . .

COLIN. He won't speak. It's a kind of singing.

MAC. Hypothermia perhaps.

HELEN. Get his jacket off.

INNES. When we were first acquent; your locks were like the raven . . .

HELEN. Towels. Colin . . . in my pack.

> *By this time,* INNES *has been ushered to the armchair.*
> *A sleeping bag is draped over him.*

INNES. Your bony brow was brent.

JACKIE. I'll offer him a whisky.

HELEN *and* COLIN. No.

MAC. That's a myth.

HELEN. Get the Primus lit. (COLIN *does this*.)

INNES (*suddenly coherent, addressing* JACKIE). You shouldn't have done that.

JACKIE. Offered you whisky?

INNES. Opened my rucksack.

MAC. That was me.

INNES. You shouldn't have done it.

MAC. We were worried. I was looking for a route-card.

INNES. I've never left a route-card in my life. You shouldn't have taken photographs.

JACKIE. Sorry.

INNES. The deil's awa, the deil's awa . . .

COLIN. He's at it again.

MAC. Which direction did he come from?

COLIN. South. I was just outside, enjoying the rain, deciding to start smoking again. I could hear bits of this song, just bits, in the wind. Then that lightning and I could see him. Striding, directly to the bothy. Not weak or stumbling. He marched past me, opened the door and fell in.

INNES. The deil's awa wi' th' Exciseman . . .

HELEN. We'll have a warm drink for you soon.

INNES. There's a kindness in you. In you all. We'll drink a cup of kindness. (COLIN *is examining the skull*.) Careful with her.

COLIN (*replacing the skull*). Just checking it's not recent. It's not.

JACKIE. It's still human bones.

HELEN. Something for your book.

MAC. No. I'm no good at describing things I've not read descriptions of. That's why you're safe too. Here, get this down you.

INNES. With just a drop. Good malt does more than Milton can, to justify God's ways to man . . .

MAC (*smiles, adds a drop of whisky*). Just a drop. Against the doctor's advice.

INNES. Absolutely. On my own head. (*Drinks.*)

HELEN. You did well to get here without a torch.

INNES. Light can blind you on the hills. I have a natural sense of direction. Even when I get lost, it's done quite naturally. This is so much more complicated now. Please, lay her to rest for the night.

HELEN. I'm not touching it.

INNES. Her, please. Not 'it'.

MAC. My job. I took her out. (MAC *replaces the skull in the rucksack.*)

JACKIE (*lightly*). Who is she, by the way?

INNES. Cauld blaws the wind frae east to west . . . a wee drop more?

HELEN. Is that sensible?

COLIN. If he's ok . . .

INNES. Of the water.

HELEN. Oh . . . of course. (INNES *pours himself more water, adds a drop of malt.*)

COLIN. If he's OK, I think I'll go to bed.

JACKIE. You're not . . . curious?

COLIN. I have a lot to think about.

MAC. Go for it. Watch the mice.

COLIN *gets his carrymat and sleeping bag and descends downstairs.*

INNES. That man has a sorrow.

JACKIE. Yes. He does.

INNES. A guilt, too.

HELEN. Does it take one to know one?

INNES. They're common bedfellows, guilt and sorrow. He has a kindness though. There's no devilment in him. I'll be off tomorrow. Will whisky douse the memory of tonight?

JACKIE. How many bottles do you have?

MAC. That's the lot.

JACKIE. Sorry. Impossible.

INNES. Ah. Ah well. Then I must take my leave in the morning.

MAC. You'll not be off tomorrow. This weather's here to stay. You need to rest. First good spell, I'll help you off.

JACKIE. He's already rescuing me. He's a hero.

INNES (*looks at* MAC). Is he now? Maybe, maybe. No, I must leave tomorrow, for Sgurr Mor.

HELEN. Why don't we see? The weather might change.

INNES. It's a wet country. The rain doesn't stop your legs from working. (*Starts to doze.*)

HELEN. You really think we're stuck? We don't have food for five.

JACKIE. Don't look at me.

MAC. There's a tin of rice pudding on the shelf.

HELEN. Shh. He's sleeping.

JACKIE. He doesn't look like a killer.

HELEN. I'm sure he's not.

JACKIE. Could be.

HELEN. We should have made him leave that downstairs.

MAC. Her. Not 'that'.

JACKIE. Your husband's downstairs.

HELEN. Well, outside then. I can't sleep with her here.

JACKIE. I can't sleep on wooden floorboards. I'm used to a mattress.

HELEN. The bones though . . . they don't bother you?

JACKIE. It's a bit . . . strange.

MAC. You'll sleep.

JACKIE. You sound confident.

MAC. You've walked a fair distance. And you don't normally. It'll take a while . . . the hard floor, the other people in the room . . . bones in the room. And your muscles. They'll be sending you messages, keeping you awake. When they're finished doing that, you'll sleep well.

JACKIE. I hope you're right.

MAC. You can borrow my sleeping bag. It's good.

JACKIE. What will you do?

MAC. I'm part of the package. There's room for two.

JACKIE. I'll take my chances with hypothermia.

MAC. I've got a bivvy bag. I'll use that.

HELEN. Everyone's just going to . . . go to bed?

JACKIE. There's not a lot else to do.

MAC. The bones don't concern us.

HELEN. Don't concern us . . . they concern me.

MAC. They don't concern us now. This minute. Because of all the things we could do, we can't do any of them now. And probably we can't do any of them tomorrow. There's a very good chance we're stuck here for a bit.

JACKIE. Stuck? In what way, stuck?

MAC. Trapped. Stormbound. Unable to get out. That way stuck.

JACKIE. It's only rain.

HELEN. It's rain that's getting worse. The forecast . . . we wouldn't have come if it hadn't been OK.

MAC (*contemptuously*). Forecasts. It's going to get worse.

Lights fade.

PART TWO

3.30 the following afternoon.

Rain. INNES *is asleep in the chair.* HELEN *adds a log to the fire.* JACKIE *is trying her phone again.*

JACKIE. I had it. I had a signal.

HELEN. You won't get it to stay. Maybe from a summit, but not from down here.

JACKIE. I'm bored. Half past three. That's twenty hours. It's like being in prison.

HELEN. It's one of those days. Heavy rain and fierce wind. The wind dies down, the mist comes down. It'll clear. At some point. Meanwhile, we've just got to sit it out.

JACKIE. I never thought I'd say this, but I think I'm going to go for a walk.

HELEN. You've no equipment. It's not safe.

JACKIE. The men are out.

HELEN. They shouldn't be. Mac's a fool.

JACKIE. He wanted to go. He's connecting with the hunter-gatherer within.

HELEN (*picking up note*). 'Weather bad. Gone to shop for supplies. Stay put. Mac.' It's absurd.

JACKIE. It's better than starving. Anyway, when you're trapped for a night and a day with an old man and a bag of bones, absurdity is a relative concept.

HELEN. We'll let the police sort that one out.

JACKIE. The police?

HELEN. I'm sure there's an explanation, but well, yes. I've thought about it. We have to tell the police.

JACKIE. We don't have to. Let's listen to him.

HELEN. He's hardly ever awake. It's a dead person. We've been sleeping next to a dead person. Or at least, you have been. I could hardly sleep at all, thinking about it.

JACKIE. I slept.

HELEN. Mac said you would. (*Pause.*) I've sent a text.

JACKIE. You got a signal?

HELEN. No. It's the advice. From the Mountain Rescue. If you can't get a signal, try a text. Sometimes it gets out. I've sent it. It's out there somewhere. Maybe it'll work.

JACKIE. Maybe your battery'll go flat first. What did you say?

HELEN. I said we wanted assistance. And I told them where we were.

JACKIE. You didn't mention . . . ?

HELEN. No. But I will. When they come.

JACKIE. If.

HELEN. Yes. If. (*Pause.*) Look, so you don't like it . . .

JACKIE. It just seems extreme.

HELEN. Someone had to do something. Mac's no use. 'Gone to shop for supplies.' Not help. Supplies.

JACKIE. I was awake when he left. We did talk about it. We just thought . . . not yet.

HELEN. She's dead.

JACKIE. She's been dead for a long time. Your husband said so. There might be a reason.

HELEN. There might not.

JACKIE. At least we know where Mac is.

HELEN. No. We know where he's going. It's different.

JACKIE. Alright. Where's Colin going? Where is he?

HELEN *walks to the window, listening to the rain.*

HELEN. Christ, I want to get out of here.

JACKIE. Thanks.

HELEN. I've left him.

Pause.

JACKIE. I'd worked that out. Your timing's great.

HELEN. He was unfaithful.

JACKIE. Whatever. He seems upset.

HELEN. I didn't think you'd understand.

JACKIE. That's obvious. You're right – I don't – but you didn't need to make it so obvious.

INNES (*who has been listening*). A horrible word, 'obvious'.

JACKIE. You're up.

INNES. No. Still prone.

HELEN. How long have you been listening?

INNES. Since I was in my youth.

HELEN. I meant just now.

INNES. I know you did. Not long.

HELEN. Did you hear me talk about getting help?

INNES. No.

HELEN. I did.

JACKIE. She's sent a text.

INNES. No matter. The police, I suspect, are not in a position to trouble me. I would hate, though, to be of trouble to them. Though to wait so long and be undone by a . . . a text . . . that would be difficult.

Pause.

HELEN. Do you want more tea?

INNES. I think it would do me good.

HELEN (*filling pan with water and lighting stove*). I am uncomfortable though, Innes.

INNES. You know my name.

HELEN. You were talking. Last night. And today. You probably don't remember. It was . . . disjointed. I'm Helen. This is Jackie. We're both . . . uncomfortable.

JACKIE. She's more uncomfortable than me.

INNES. Jackie . . . you take photographs.

JACKIE. I've erased them.

INNES. It's not good for a photographer to get uncomfortable too easily. The world is rotten, but it goes at pace. If your job is to freeze it, you might see things that are better unseen.

HELEN. You've a dead person in your rucksack. That's what's making me uncomfortable.

INNES. I regret that. Although a human death should still have the power to upset, I regret that it is you that is in that position. The gentleman was quite wrong to . . . to unveil it.

JACKIE. He wishes he hadn't.

INNES. He apologised, I seem to remember. Like I said, a gentleman. I think he is enamoured of you.

JACKIE. No . . . he saved my life. Probably. He feels protective.

INNES. He's gone to the shops. To try and get you bagels.

JACKIE (*embarrassed*). You were awake? (INNES *nods.*) You heard me promise him a . . .

INNES. A reward was specified, yes. But a gentleman would not insist on collecting.

JACKIE. It wasn't serious. He understood that. It's . . . it's the way my friends speak.

HELEN. Casually.

JACKIE. Yes. Casually.

HELEN. I'm sure . . . I'm sure there's an explanation. But at the moment – as things stand – I'm still uncomfortable. And if I could get a signal, I'd call the police.

INNES. You can spend your life waiting for a signal. Please, do not think of her.

JACKIE. This place is so small. And outside is so big. I feel like I'm suffocating in here. Put a corpse in the corner and my mind does turn towards it.

HELEN. I'm not sure it counts as a corpse anymore. But yes, it's difficult to ignore.

INNES. The other man last night. He is your husband?

HELEN. Yes. Colin.

INNES. He slept downstairs?

HELEN. Yes. I don't know where he is now.

JACKIE. Are you worried?

HELEN. A bit concerned, yes.

INNES. I'm sorry, I need to close my eyes again. I must leave here fairly soon. Rest is important.

JACKIE. He can't leave before Mac gets back.

HELEN. *If* Mac gets back. Even if he wants to, maybe he can't.

JACKIE. How far's the shop?

HELEN. Depends. He might head for Loch Quoich or take his chances in Glen Dessary. Either way, he's got a substantial walk over rough terrain and then he's hoping to hitch, I presume. You can see why booking into a hotel in Invergarry might seem more attractive than attempting the return leg.

JACKIE. He'll come back.

HELEN. Everyone's got a lot of faith in him.

JACKIE. He's left his pack.

HELEN. True. He'll come back for that. But maybe not today. Nobody else can lift it, let alone steal it.

JACKIE. He's got a beautiful blue rock in there. He'll come back.

HELEN. He *says* he's got a beautiful blue rock in there. It sounds utterly implausible to me.

JACKIE. You're not in a trusting place at the moment.

HELEN. I trusted Colin. I trusted him absolutely. But he lied. He had a choice – stay true to what he'd promised or throw it away to get inside the pants of an eighteen-year- old art student. (*To* INNES.) Sorry.

INNES. You're angry.

JACKIE. How old's Colin?

HELEN. Thirty-six.

JACKIE. Twice her age. I've heard worse.

HELEN. It was five years ago.

Pause.

JACKIE. So this is just . . . bickering.

HELEN. No. He's only just found out.

JACKIE. That you know?

INNES. That he's not forgiven. I'm right?

HELEN. We were supposed to climb our last Munro together. Today.

JACKIE. And you've left him.

HELEN (*upset, but holding it in*). Yes. And I've climbed it before.

JACKIE. I don't quite get this.

HELEN. When he begged to come back, we . . . we ended up climbing the Munros together. But I'd done this one first.

JACKIE. Doing the Munros takes five years?

HELEN. We were out every weekend we could get free. It's a big thing.

JACKIE. I guess what I'm asking is . . . are you a complete bitch?

INNES. Please.

HELEN. I know . . . I know adultery happens. I'm not naïve. But when I found out . . . nothing prepared me for how I felt. When I was seventeen, I was knocked down by a car. Finding out what Colin had been doing was exactly the same. I was physically sore. Every bone and muscle in my body ached. I felt sick and I couldn't move. I lived with a headache like your worst hangover for three weeks. When I thought, I hurt. When that was finished, I cried. And then, one of my friends told me it was only a fling. That was when I thought throwing him out was too easy. I wanted him to feel something of how I felt, that sudden anaphylactic shock of the ground you thought was solid disappearing beneath you, just when you thought it was firm.

Pause.

JACKIE. And was it worth it?

HELEN. You're a photographer. It's your job to capture moments – this has been five years. I can't . . . reduce that to a yes or no.

JACKIE. Two hundred and eighty-four mountains and five years living with someone you don't love. And you don't know if it was worth it?

HELEN. I never said I didn't love him. I said – I was trying to say – I wanted to hurt him.

They sit for a while, drinking whisky.

JACKIE. I wish Mac would get back.

HELEN. He likes you too.

JACKIE. It's his food I'm after. It's not as if there's much to do in here.

HELEN. There's more than that. Maybe not much more, but something.

JACKIE. He frustrates me. He'll never write a book about this trip. Even I know that's been done twenty times before. You need more than a rock. How can you write about landscape when you're charging through it with your head down?

HELEN. I suppose you don't write about landscape. You write about charging through it.

JACKIE. Your guide to the Munros. That's one I'd read.

HELEN. Mine?

JACKIE. I've never been up one. But I saw them yesterday. And I just can't see it. They . . . I'm aware I'm alone on this, but I just don't find them beautiful. But I imagine, when you get to the top, there is a feeling – some sort of elation. And I know with some of them it's just a slog up a big, round lump of heather. But at the top, there must be something. But what you felt at each summit – that would be interesting. Anger, a vengeful thrill, or did you forget? Did you just celebrate?

HELEN. You can't hold on to revenge forever. I learnt that.

The sound of the downstairs door opening.

JACKIE. It's Mac.

HELEN. Or Colin.

MAC (*from below*). It's both. (MAC *appears.*) Mission accomplished. (*Lies on floor and reaches down to take three carrier bags from* COLIN.) They didn't have bagels.

JACKIE. Bad luck.

MAC (*gesturing to* INNES). Is he all right?

INNES (*eyes closed*). I'm fine, thank you, Mac. I'm sorry about the bagels. Though perhaps it's for the best.

MAC (*disconcerted*). Come on, Colin.

COLIN (*from below*). I'm fine down here.

MAC. It's cold down there. (*To* HELEN.) Given the conditions, and the fact that you've not quite managed to let the fire go out, we should all be up here. Agreed?

HELEN. Of course. Where was he?

MAC. The other side of the col. I think he'd tried to climb Sgurr Mor. You'd think he'd wait for you. Here. (*Throws* JACKIE *a packet of cigarettes.*) Share those between you. But I still don't approve. (*To* COLIN.) Stop being daft. It's toasty up here.

COLIN. It's OK down here . . . not too cold.

JACKIE. What else did you get? (*Empties one polythene bag on table – various tins fall out – soup and fruit. Also a cauliflower, some cheese.*)

HELEN. Colin. Please come up. (*No answer.* INNES *gets up – a bit shaky – and goes down the ladder.*)

MAC. Are you all right there?

INNES. Fine. I've been sitting down too long, that's all. Nature calls and the body must respond.

JACKIE. A cauliflower.

MAC. Good to have something fresh.

JACKIE. I know, but a fucking cauliflower.

MAC. There's cheese too. You can see my thinking. There's pre-pack sandwiches as well though – I figured you'd want something straight away.

HELEN. You made very good time. Seven hours or so. How?

MAC. Later. Bag number three. Whisky and vodka. (*Reaches into his pocket.*) Bag number four – I'm quite proud of this one. (*Holds up a cellophane bag of grass.*)

HELEN. We're stormbound and you pop out to the shops and manage to buy drugs? You're making a mockery out of the whole thing.

MAC (*as* JACKIE *takes the bag and begins to construct a joint*). I'll be barman. Large Highland Parks all round?

JACKIE. This looks like good stuff. How did you get it?

MAC. Got a lift from two ghillies. It's always worth asking.

JACKIE. Did you get a lift back as well?

MAC. Kind of. Taxi.

HELEN. A taxi?

MAC. Seemed the obvious move. There's always taxis. If you're on a road, anywhere in the Highlands, there's somebody, somewhere, who'll pick you up and drive you somewhere else if you give them money. You just need their number. And a phone-box. Makes a huge difference.

HELEN. Only on Mull.

MAC. Sorry?

HELEN. No transport, except for Mull. You said.

MAC. Ah. Yes. I did. I did say that.

INNES *and* COLIN *return.*

INNES. Just sit. Any seat. No need for anyone to change the subject.

MAC. I kind of wanted to.

HELEN. We were just talking about Mac's continuous Munro trip. You know, the one without any transport. And the fact that it's a load of bollocks.

COLIN (*to* MAC). You lied?

JACKIE. So did your wife.

INNES. Jackie. That will not do.

MAC. I did lie. Sometimes the weight just . . . hurts. It's painful. When you're on a hill, tough. You just have to keep going. But it's the road miles that sap your will. When it's suddenly possible not to carry it . . . to hitch a lift or phone a cab . . . yes. Sometimes I cheat.

JACKIE. It might be a better book. People like failures.

MAC. There won't be a book. We both know that.

INNES. The originals. They used taxis. Hired hands from the estates to transport their gear, or a pony and trap to make Glen Tilt a little easier. But they could walk. Those gentlemen could walk.

MAC. And they were breaking new ground. There's nothing left to do now. Continuous Munros, Munros and tops, Munros in winter . . . Corbetts and Grahams thrown in . . . it's all been done. It's getting boring. Who wants to read another book on the same hills, by someone who took a blue rock up them? You're right, it may as well be a fridge.

JACKIE. It's not the rock, it's the insight.

MAC. I don't have any insight. You've seen Gairich. The hill I found you on. You think it's wilderness. It's not. There's no new way to describe it. Five thousand people have stood at that summit and most of them have written about it – books, logs, bothy visitor books, postcards . . . There's no new language. You know A'Bhuidheanach Bheag?

HELEN. Not the most exciting.

MAC. You could practically drive up most of the height gain. Then a saunter along to the trig point. We do it because it's on a list. No other reason. I'd climb Arthur's Seat for a view, for fun or whatever. But A' Bhuidheanach Bheag's shit. Dalwhinnie. It makes me angry.

COLIN. We got lost on it. (MAC *looks incredulous.*) It's a flat summit. Lots of mist. It can be tricky.

HELEN. He broke his arm on Ben Chonzie. We specialise in finding ways of remembering the dull ones. But you're right, Mac. They're not all great and they've certainly been written about too much. If anyone can help you, it's Jackie.

JACKIE. Me?

HELEN. You've never been up a hill. Never read a book about them. You might . . . might see them in a new way. Your photographs of a Munro-round plagued by doubt and dishonesty – the combination might make a book.

JACKIE (*lighting the joint*). Interesting idea. But you've got to understand, I really, really want to go home. I'm hating it here.

Silence.

MAC. Cauliflower cheese. That'll cheer you up.

Lights fade.

PART THREE

Later that evening, after the meal.

JACKIE *passes a joint to* MAC. MAC *accepts.*

HELEN. I thought you didn't smoke in bothies.

MAC. We've established I have a cavalier attitude towards my own rules.

JACKIE. You've a cavalier attitude towards cooking, we've established that.

MAC. I knew I'd get no thanks.

INNES. Yet you know we're all grateful.

JACKIE. Parboiled cauliflower with cheese on top.

MAC. 'Parboiled' makes it sound like a recipe. Thanks.

HELEN. It's food. That's the important thing. I think we should make a move tomorrow. Whatever happens. Leave Sgurr Mor unclimbed – it'll still be there later. Take the bones back . . .

INNES. I wonder . . . (*They all look at him, expecting a revelation.*)

COLIN. Yes?

INNES. I wonder if I might share your drugs.

MAC (*laughs, passing the joint*). Of course.

JACKIE. I didn't even think . . . Sorry, Innes.

INNES. Not at all. I don't usually. But sometimes – not often, but sometimes – I find it gives me clarity.

MAC. The opposite with me. I go all over the place. Which is why I never touch the stuff.

JACKIE. I know what you mean. It can make you hung up on something, so much so that you explore it from every angle,

obsessively. Seeing it in new ways. Later, you've either
nailed the problem or you've realised it isn't a problem.

HELEN (*to* INNES). Is that what you're doing? Working
through a problem?

COLIN. Leave him.

INNES. That's all right. Yes. I'm addressing a problem. You
see, it's quite impossible for me to take Elspeth back to
Ayrshire. If the weather doesn't change . . . well, I can't
take her back, I can't leave her here . . .

MAC. I got a Met forecast. It's not good news.

HELEN. We could make it out. It's not too far to the road.
Difficult but doable. But anything else would be madness.

COLIN. We've found summits in worse than this.

HELEN. Only because we were caught out. We've never
started in weather like this.

COLIN. Glen Affric.

HELEN. We didn't know what we were doing. And we almost
died.

INNES. I still don't know what I'm doing.

JACKIE. And she is dead.

INNES. Quite. At some point this mist will clear. Met forecast
or not. I must wait. When it clears, I will leave. I have to
bury Elspeth on top of a hill.

Silence.

JACKIE. Who is she?

INNES. I suspect she would be secretly pleased to be spoken
about all this time later. As you know, this is Elspeth. And
she died fifty years ago. Fifty years and almost a month
now . . . I've been prevaricating. She was a kind of mother
to a lot of us. And we all believed in her. And her religion.
She had . . . strange beliefs.

JACKIE. It was a cult?

INNES. Now, certainly, that's what they would call it. I think,
though, it was only a delusion.

JACKIE. What did she believe?

MAC. So many questions.

INNES. Perhaps I owe you this. So much later, her beliefs
seem . . . addled. I can't remember them all. But there was
the matter . . . (*almost a giggle*) the small matter of her
immortality. (*Pause.*) As you can see she was wrong. (*They
look at the rucksack.*) No matter, on her deathbed she told
us she was . . . going up to wait for us. She'd come back,
she said. Come back to get us. In a week.

JACKIE. But she didn't.

INNES. We hadn't had enough belief. Which meant we had to
wait for a year. Some, of course, just gave up, and those that
knew her best gave her a burial. A couple of lads dug her up
though and we waited another year. For another reprimand.
Not enough faith. Her last condition tested us beyond our
limits. We were to wait fifty years. Fifty years of unyielding
devotion and she'd come down and take us to heaven. I'm
afraid she asked too much. Nobody lasted another full year.

HELEN. Except you.

INNES. God, no. I've been an atheist for . . . well, forty-nine
years now. No, I . . . I realised quite early on, it was . . .
unlikely she'd be coming back. But somehow, underneath
all the Old Testament sermonising, there was the stuff of a
decent person there. I stopped believing her, but I never
stopped believing that she believed. It seemed unfair to leave
her in a shallow grave in an Ayrshire outhouse. I promised
her I'd come back, after the fifty years, and if the miracle
hadn't happened, I'd give her a decent burial. There might
not be a heaven, but the top of a Scottish mountain comes
pretty close.

HELEN. Why Sgurr Mor?

INNES. I knew there'd be a spade. And I thought it would be
quiet. (*Pause.*) I had no wish to talk so much. I insist you let
me wash up.

COLIN. Leave it. We can wait and see about tomorrow, but
just now even going to the burn's out of the question.

INNES. You've been out once today. I haven't. In your
own very different ways, I value your company greatly.

Please . . . don't misinterpret my very real desire to escape from it for a time.

COLIN. At least let me help you.

JACKIE. Someone should go with you. I rolled that quite strong.

INNES. You did, yes. For the best, for the best.

MAC. I'd do them, but I cooked. It would be wrong to hog all the good jobs.

INNES. Why not, Colin? Thank you. Yes, you can help me.

COLIN. I'll get my torch.

MAC. Here. Borrow this. It cost a fortune but it's good. Totally wind and rainproof. It's not even on the market. Better than Gore-tex.

INNES (*putting on his own waterproof, that looks like a macintosh*). Better than Gore-tex, is it? They do some clever things these days. Yet I fancy this will do the trick. Are we ready, Colin?

COLIN. I think so. I've got a compass. And a whistle. I know it's not far . . .

HELEN. No, you're quite right. Look after each other. (INNES *leaves first. It takes* COLIN *a bit of time to collect everything into a plastic basin and negotiate it downstairs.*)

JACKIE. I've heard of Gore-tex.

HELEN. It's a waterproofing system.

MAC. He's quite right though. Too many upgrades. Stick to what works. Here, you go first, I'll hand it to you. (*Assists* COLIN.)

The door downstairs opens. The volume of wind and rain increases.

COLIN (*from below*). Christ, it's bad out there.

INNES (*from below*). Then relish it, Colin. Relish it. (*The sound of the door shutting.* MAC *hangs up his waterproofs.*)

MAC. I'd give anything to have gear as old as his. Never to have heard of GPS.

JACKIE. Should we have let him go?

HELEN. I was hoping it'll change his mind about going up Sgurr Mor tomorrow.

MAC. Nothing's going to change his mind.

JACKIE (*pouring herself a drink*). I'm drinking too fast. Somebody tell me to slow down.

HELEN. Slow down.

JACKIE. Thanks.

HELEN (*pours herself a drink*). I feel . . . exhausted.

MAC. Always the same when you do nothing all day.

HELEN. I just didn't expect it to be like this.

JACKIE. You're not as surprised as Colin.

MAC. He's holding it together quite well. Under the circumstances.

JACKIE. He is not. He's devastated.

HELEN. You both speak as though you know him.

JACKIE (*quietly*). I know he didn't deserve this.

HELEN. Deserve this or deserve me?

JACKIE (*to* MAC). She's been up Sgurr Mor. She's done them all.

Pause.

MAC. I thought it was something like that. When are you going to tell him?

HELEN. He knows.

MAC. Like I said, he's holding up quite well. (*Holds up glass.*) Congratulations.

HELEN. I don't need sarcasm.

MAC. You've completed. It's a hell of an achievement. What was your last one?

HELEN. Beinn Mhanach.

MAC. Not the best. Not the worst though. A bit underrated.

HELEN. Not as classy as A' Mhaighdean.

MAC. Now there's a hill to finish on.

HELEN. It took us two-and-a-half days, walking in from
Poolewe, camping by the Dubh Loch. On the way up to the
summit, the weather changed. Colin was struggling – some
kind of viral thing he thought he'd got rid of. I must have
been twenty minutes ahead. I stopped about eighty metres
short of the cairn, managed to light a cigarette and waited.
When Colin appeared, I told him I'd already been up, and
I'd wait for him. I lit another cigarette, he summitted,
rejoined me and we went down together.

Pause.

JACKIE. So you haven't done them all.

HELEN. I've done all the ones I'm going to do.

MAC. Would you do Sgurr Mor again though?

HELEN. Why? Why would I want to do that?

JACKIE. To help Innes.

HELEN. I'm not sure I believed all that. No, I won't go up
Sgurr Mor.

JACKIE. At least cancel your text.

HELEN. The battery's dead. So you trust him?

JACKIE. I think so.

MAC. One hundred per cent. Even if he hadn't told us, we had
to help him. You heard what the man said. He's not taking
her back. And he may have a lot of quiet strength but I
wouldn't put money on him getting to the top of Sgurr Mor,
not even in sunshine. He took a hell of a soaking yesterday.
Your escape plan tomorrow's good, but we can't leave him
here.

HELEN. If he refuses to come with us what choice do we
have?

JACKIE. A simple one. We leave without him, or we stay and
help him.

HELEN. You want to go back. You hate it here.

JACKIE. Yes, I want to go back. I find this unbearable, like a prison. It's so confined . . . and outside is so desolate. I'm glad I've come. It's good to know what being really trapped is like. I don't like it, and I know all the times I've said I was trapped or stuck or whatever . . . well, I'll choose different words next time. For the last thirty hours, I've had no choices to make. Maybe that's what being trapped is. Now we have a choice to make, it's completely different. And I'm not going to choose to leave him here.

HELEN. I didn't mean leave him here. I meant . . . if we call his bluff, surely he'll come with us. We say we're leaving, surely he'll come with us.

MAC. I don't think Innes . . . I mean I don't know anything about him but I don't think he's someone who bluffs. And if he's not bluffing, we can't call it. Also . . . he made a promise. A stupid one, but he intends to keep it. It's honourable. I like that.

HELEN. I have to leave here tomorrow. I can't stay here.

JACKIE. It's like I said. Lack of choice. All the time you were climbing those hills, you were choosing. You almost chose not to go through with it, you've committed now. You're trapped.

MAC. Not yet. You could save this. If you wanted. I've never been in a marriage, but . . . I look at you and Colin, and I think . . . what chance do I have if you two can't make it work?

JACKIE. Really?

HELEN. You don't agree.

JACKIE. Maybe. I don't know . . . I just think you went too far.

HELEN. Maybe I did. A lot of my friends are marrying now. They've reached a certain stage and whoever they're with becomes the one. It wasn't like that with me. I married the first person I fell in love with. I was eighteen, he was twenty. We married four years later. That's nine years of my life he took up before he . . . before he made his decisions. Leaving the city, climbing hills . . . the life we took up was supposed to be difficult for him. But he loves it. Yes. You're right. I went too far. But he'll recover.

MAC (*goes to his rucksack and takes out a polythene bag. Inside is a beautiful blue rock*). Look at this.

JACKIE. The beautiful blue rock.

MAC. Do you like it?

HELEN. It's . . . lovely.

JACKIE. Yes. I do.

MAC. Needs a polish. It's actually bluer than it looks just now. Sometimes, if I can be bothered, I push it into a summit cairn and take a photograph. Mostly I just carry it.

HELEN. Why?

MAC. I don't know. I thought I was finding out. Listening to Jackie talking about being trapped, I thought, maybe that's the point of the rock. I've always got the choice to leave it behind. It makes all that weight seem . . . optional. But now I'm looking at it, that doesn't seem right. I think it's because it's . . . beautiful. It's not special. I bought it in Bergen, in a market stall that sold beautiful rocks. It even looked a bit tame there, surrounded by all those other even bigger, even brighter ones. But I thought, well, if you came across that in Torridon it would be amazing. Absolutely amazing. So I bought it. And it looked great in Torridon. But it wasn't just the rock that looked great. Torridon looked fantastic. All of a sudden I could see how dark it was. Different greys, of rock and cloud, green and brown. Sometimes when things are a bit shit, this helps me find the beauty in all that mess. So it's right that it's heavy. Something this useful shouldn't be easy.

HELEN. Is that why it's out now? To help you find something beautiful in a mess? (*The sound of the door opening.*)

JACKIE. They're coming back.

MAC. We look after Innes. Right? Unconditionally. We don't force him back to Ayrshire, and we give Elspeth a decent burial. We make sure he's safe, and that means not leaving him here. Then you and Colin, you go your separate ways. Or you don't.

COLIN (*appearing at the hatch with the basin of washing*).
   We're pretty wet. We'll take the waterproofs off downstairs.

HELEN. I'll put the stove on.

COLIN. Thanks. What's that?

JACKIE. It's a rock.

COLIN. It's nice. (*Goes downstairs. MAC replaces the rock in his rucksack. HELEN lights the stove.*)

JACKIE (*to HELEN*). The one you didn't climb.

HELEN. A' Mhaighdean.

JACKIE. Yes.

HELEN. What about it?

JACKIE. Don't tell Colin.

HELEN. Why not?

JACKIE. I just think it makes it worse. (INNES *appears and glances at his rucksack.*)

INNES. A bracing experience, as washing-up goes.

JACKIE. Are you OK?

INNES. Better for being out.

   COLIN *appears.*

COLIN. Did you hear the helicopter?

JACKIE. No. Are we being rescued?

COLIN. That's what I wondered. Where did you tell your friends you were going?

JACKIE. Just . . . up north.

COLIN. It's not us, then. They're just going through the motions anyway. Hoping for a flare. There's no chance of a rescue tonight. It's hell out there.

HELEN. Which makes it madness to stay tomorrow. One quiet patch, even if it's still raining, and we should be off.

INNES. As I scrubbed that pan, I wondered . . . Well, as I scrubbed that pan, I wondered why it was necessary to melt the cheese on to the cauliflower while it was in the pan. It

could just as well have happened in our individual plates –
cleaning would have been a lot easier. Then I thought, what
a fine parcel o' rogues to be stuck in a bothy with. What
fun. What craik we could have another night. But whenever
you forget about her, Elspeth has a way of entering your
thoughts. There always was a slightly . . . selfish side to her.
Helen, Mac, Jackie . . . thank you for your kindness . . . no,
your forbearance. You're right to leave tomorrow. (*Coughs
badly.*) I only ask you to forgive an old man his
peculiarities, and to put me out of your thoughts.

HELEN. She's dead, Innes. We can't forget.

INNES. Aye, dead. And I didn't kill her. So let me bury her.

MAC. We'll do more than that. We'll help you.

INNES. You're a good man, Mac. But that won't be necessary.

MAC. We'd already decided. I opened your rucksack. It's the
least I can do.

COLIN. I'm helping him. (*Silence.*) I'm going up there
anyway. All three of us. (*Gestures to the third, Elspeth.*) We
all want to bag the same summit. I thought about not
bothering, but well, I'm here. I may as well. I asked Innes if
he would let me . . . assist. In the event of bad weather
continuing. Carry the spade, dig a hole. That sort of thing.

INNES. It was a very kind offer. Readily accepted.

COLIN. You're helping me. Tomorrow would have been . . .
difficult. It has its own purpose now.

INNES. And we may compromise a little. Place her just a little
away from the summit proper. I don't believe the police
would be wanting to do too much digging up there.

HELEN. This is absurd. Don't even think about it.

JACKIE. I'll come too. Stop telling us what's right and wrong.

HELEN. I wasn't talking about morals. I was talking about
weather. We've got the chance to get back tomorrow
morning, that might not be possible in the afternoon.

INNES. There's no need for you to come, Jackie. But thank
you.

COLIN. You take the car, Helen. I'll find my own way back, pick up a few things . . . you know.

HELEN. You've made up your mind?

COLIN. When we started this . . . we knew it wasn't always safe. We've always calculated risk, balanced it with reward. This is no different.

HELEN. Where will you go?

COLIN. No point in grand gestures. I'll stay in Galashiels for a while. Work out my notice. Then take off. Maybe try and get a warder's job, with a hostel. Start trying to live in the land instead of just pushing through it all the time.

MAC. Well, good luck.

JACKIE. Yes. Good luck.

MAC. We've a few things to drink to. One more?

INNES. An excellent idea.

JACKIE. What about you?

HELEN. Yes. Why not?

JACKIE. I didn't mean a drink. What are you going to do now?

MAC. We've all got decisions to make. Doesn't do to be put on the spot.

JACKIE. We'll never see each other again. I'm not going to hold her to anything. Anyway, what decisions have you got to make?

MAC. I don't know. I just sense that I have.

JACKIE. So . . .

HELEN. Are you asking out of concern, or are you turning the screw?

JACKIE (*pauses*). I suspect I'm turning the screw. Ignore me.

HELEN. I'm moving to Ireland.

COLIN. Ireland? We don't know anyone in Ireland.

HELEN. But it's got beautiful mountains and I won't need to learn a new language. That's three things it's got going for it.

I just . . . I just need a break. To work out what it all means. I'm sorry, Colin. I should have done this five years ago. I don't like the world I've been living in.

They all have a drink by now.

COLIN. To Carn Dearg. (*Raises glass.*)

MAC. Which one?

COLIN. By Rannoch.

HELEN. Don't.

MAC. Doubled it with Sgor Gaibhre, I suspect. Then down for an overnight in Ben Alder?

COLIN. No. We did it on its own.

HELEN. Here we go.

COLIN. Had to go back five years later for Sgor Gaibhre, of course. No. We wanted to stay somewhere nice afterwards. It was our first one. My first one anyway. There's a hotel by Rannoch Station. We stayed there. A long walk in – at least it felt like it then. On the old Road to the Isles. A ruin. I remember a ruin. We pulled up the west side of Carn Dearg – not much view. When we got to the top, it just lifted. All I could see in every direction was hills. When I've finished these, I thought, I'm going to come back here and I'm going to be able to name every single hill. After dinner, in bed, I really thought this might work. You had me fooled.

INNES. To Carn Dearg, then.

COLIN. Not just to Carn Dearg. After that, Ben Oss and Beinn Dubhchraig, Schiehallion, Meall Chuaich, Meall nan Tarmachan, Lochnagar, Ben Cruachan, Stob Diamh, Stuchd an Lochan.

HELEN. Ten will do. Please.

COLIN. Three years on. Number one hundred and forty-two. The halfway point, reached on the Cuillin ridge.

HELEN. Yes. We went up those hills. Together. And now we're here.

COLIN. I think we were together. I need to know if I'm right. On that boat to Knoydart. Lost in Fisherfield. An Teallach . . .

Torridon weekends, Glen Affric, Corrour Lodge. Watching an avalanche on Meall a' Chrasgaidh. New Year on Wyvis. Ben Lomond to Ben Hope, Ben More to Mount Keen . . .

HELEN. Mount Keen . . .

COLIN. It was a misty day. It's a featureless lump. But we were still on a hill. The air was clean. The wind . . . our faces hurt with the wind. You can't open your lungs. And if you could shout, no-one would hear you. Your voice just goes . . . So all you do is walk. Walk on till it's over. And because you can't talk with anyone, you just walk with them. It's . . . pure. All the hills we walked up without seeing anything – all the viewpoints with no view . . . in Glencoe, Glen Etive, on Beinn Eighe and in Kintail . . . there was still that. That purity of walking. With you. It must have meant something.

HELEN. The years we were together before we climbed a hill – I thought that meant something.

COLIN. You're on every page of every logbook. You're in every photograph of a summit cairn or a trig point. You're in every memory of the Scottish hills that I've got.

Pause.

INNES. Not to Carn Dearg, then. But to the purity of walking. And all the hills you mentioned. All of them.

HELEN. And A' Mhaighdean. (*A look from* JACKIE.)

MAC. And to you, Innes.

INNES. No, not to me.

MAC. Yes. You're a walker. Old-school. No Munro maps, no collecting. Just the hills.

JACKIE. I'm with Mac. And if we're not drinking to you, then we're drinking to my idea of you. There's nothing about being here that makes me want to spend my weekends climbing hills and ticking lists. Nothing. I'll stay in the city. But I look at my friends, and me, and we seem . . . insubstantial. Exhibition openings, gigs, lines of coke in club toilets, guest passes. Projects. Everyone's always working on a project. No-one has the confidence to say nothing. To just go about their business (*Looks at Elspeth.*) – whatever that is.

INNES. Whatever that is . . . Thank you, Jackie, for overestimating me. If we must raise glasses, let it be for those that used to live here.

JACKIE. Here?

INNES. This was the byre. They lived twenty yards away. And others lived that way and that way. It was a community. The glen was alive with people. No Gore-tex. No summits ticked off. Man and nature, together. Not always peacefully, but together. And, I think, with dignity. The people who lived here may have lied, cheated, stolen. I don't know. But the situation had dignity. This isn't a wilderness. But the only reason we sometimes think that it is, is because we made it that way. The reason to walk, for me, has always been to connect back to that time. When you're standing on a summit, if you're lucky enough to have a view, you're looking at ghost towns in the glens below.

COLIN. To ghost towns.

JACKIE. I thought you'd toast Elspeth.

INNES. She didn't drink. It seemed inappropriate. Now please, talk on. Though remember, Mac, I can't promise not to be listening just because my eyes are shut.

MAC. Bloody bagels. No, sleep's good. An early start's your best chance tomorrow.

Lights fade as they prepare to sleep.

PART FOUR

11.30 the next morning.

It is still raining, but not as heavily. HELEN *is sweeping up.* INNES *is sleeping. The rest have gone.* INNES *awakes, sits up and watches* HELEN.

INNES. Where's Elspeth?

HELEN. You're awake, then.

INNES. I think so. The others . . .

HELEN (*stops sweeping*). Away. To Sgurr Mor. With Elspeth.

INNES. They shouldn't have done that.

HELEN. You gave them your blessing.

INNES. I did?

HELEN. Yes. 'I give you my blessing.' That's what you said.

INNES. I'm not a religious man. My blessing has no meaning.

HELEN. It's all they had to go on. Look, obviously you don't remember. They woke you, you got up, fell, tried again, fell again. You were shivering – the fire was still going, everyone else was still too hot. You're . . . you're not well. Probably just a chill. Even getting to the car's going to be tough. They're going to carry you. Sgurr Mor was out of the question. You wouldn't have made it.

INNES. When did they leave?

HELEN. Four hours ago. They'll be back soon. It's almost twelve. You've been out for fourteen hours. Well. Kind of out. You've been speaking quite a bit.

INNES. Sorry.

HELEN. Don't worry. Nothing that made any sense. Some Burns' poems – snatches of them anyway. Old songs. That kind of thing. It was like having Radio Scotland on with bad reception.

INNES. Jackie went too?

HELEN. She insisted. She's going to take a photograph for you.

INNES. There's no need for that. It's no weather to be introducing somebody to the joys of walking the hills.

HELEN. I know. They tried to talk her out of it. But she'd been stuck in here a long time. But she said taking a photograph for you meant leaving her camera here.

HELEN. Does this count, then? Have you done what you set out to do?

INNES. I don't know. I promised to bury her. I haven't. On the other hand, she's been buried.

HELEN. Well, not all of her.

INNES. What do you mean?

HELEN. I'm afraid I found a thumb. I think it's a thumb. When I was sweeping up. It must have fallen out that first night, when Mac opened the rucksack.

INNES. Let me see.

HELEN *hands over an outdoor magazine, onto which she has swept the thumb.* INNES *picks it up.*

INNES. Were they going to bury the Bible with her?

HELEN. Yes . . . I think. Everything together, in the rucksack. That was the plan.

INNES. A good book, the Bible. She liked all the wrong bits.

HELEN. I've never read it.

INNES. Not many people have.

HELEN. What do you want to do about the thumb?

INNES. I don't know.

HELEN. We could bury it here. If you like. You could say a few words.

INNES. A few words . . . Do bones burn?

HELEN. I . . . I guess so.

INNES. They must do. The very basis of cremation. A few words . . . Elspeth, I made you a promise. I've not quite kept to it, but you'll have to live with that. You know what I mean. Also . . . your influence waned. But a promise is a promise for right or wrong. In your prime, you were quite persuasive. Your thumb's getting cremated. Sorry about that. (*He tosses the thumb into the fire, quite casually, and turns to* HELEN.) I suspect you don't consider any of what I said last night to be much of an explanation. I can't offer much more.

HELEN. That's all right.

INNES. I thought you'd understand.

HELEN. I don't. Understand, that is. I've just decided to accept. In this instance.

INNES. People keep asking you for explanations as well.

HELEN. They feel they're entitled, I suppose.

INNES. But you never explained.

HELEN. I explained as much as I could. Some of it . . . I can't explain it all.

INNES. The simplest things are the hardest to explain. Right now, Mac and Colin are probably trying to explain to Jackie why they like this. She'll be wet, cold . . . she won't have had a view . . . and they won't be able to explain what it is that to them – and you – is so vital about walking up and down hills.

HELEN. I know.

INNES. The first time I came across a copy of the New Testament – after I'd left home – the only part that left any impression was the forty days and forty nights in the wilderness. I remember thinking, as the drill sergeant shouted, how much more preferable that sounded to most of my existence. That need to walk in big empty spaces . . . don't explain it. Just do it.

HELEN. You don't believe I've been doing a good . . . a healthy thing for the last five years. I know you don't.

INNES. I know you can't explain it. So perhaps . . . in some way . . . you had to do it. The desire to walk is simple. But walking itself is never so. Cliffs that look impossible but you climb them in minutes, flat ground that's uncrossable bog. The deaths you get on a clear summer's day.

HELEN. When I'm walking . . . I know what you mean, but it's when I'm walking that things seem clear. Simple, if you like. On Monday morning, back at work, that's when everything seems so . . . difficult again. It's the same stuff that I'm thinking about. It seems clear when I'm walking and difficult the next day. That's my problem with mountains. What Colin says about . . . I don't know . . . sunsets over Beinn Alligan . . . of course it's beautiful. Of course I felt that. But mountains make you think things are easier than they are.

INNES. Yes. That might be the point of them.

HELEN. Are you alright?

INNES. Just tired. Very tired.

HELEN. I made a flask up. (*She pours a cup from it.*) It's just hot water. We've run out of coffee.

INNES. Have we run out of Highland Park?

HELEN. Is that a good idea?

INNES. I can't explain it, so in some elemental way, it probably is.

HELEN. Help yourself. I haven't packed it. I thought the grave-digging Munro-baggers might feel the need for a dram.

INNES. Oh, I'm sure they will. (*Pours himself a measure. The sound of the door opening downstairs.*)

MAC (*from below*). Whisky! Give me whisky!

INNES. And if there were any doubt . . .

MAC (*appearing*). Not that I need it. But it's not been a cakewalk out there. We're all pretty wet.

HELEN. Help yourself. The other two?

MAC. Not far behind. It's all done. We . . . we didn't know what you wanted really. Probably we should have said a few words or something. But it was pretty miserable up there. By the time we'd rebuilt the cairn, well . . . we just said bye and shuffled off.

INNES. You know exactly where she's buried now.

MAC. Shit.

HELEN. Don't worry.

INNES. I won't.

MAC. Are you OK? The weather's bad, but better than yesterday. It's time to make a break for it.

INNES. With your help and sufferance.

MAC. I . . . I buried my beautiful blue rock with her. Not in the rucksack, but in the cairn. I hope you don't mind.

INNES. Not at all. I would have liked to have seen this rock, but in a way, I'm glad you've let go of it.

HELEN. Why? I was beginning to understand why you carry it, and now you've got rid of it.

MAC. You're right. I really liked it. But it's a bit stupid, backpacking with a rock.

HELEN. And the continuous . . . are you carrying on?

MAC. I'm still going to go up hills. But no . . . I'm going to sea-kayak round Scotland instead. No taxis to tempt me. Then I'll have to go back to work. The money's running out. All this back-to-nature stuff. It's all got to be paid for.

HELEN. Well, good luck.

MAC. Thanks. First, I've got to overcome a fear of the sea. Then learn to kayak. It could take a while. (*The sound of the door opening downstairs.*)

That's them.

JACKIE (*from below*). Don't even think of setting straight off.

MAC. We've got a gap in the weather. Shouldn't hang around.

JACKIE (*appearing through hatch*). I'm having a drink. End of story.

HELEN. Help yourself. (JACKIE *pours a vodka.* COLIN *appears.*)

INNES. Thank you. Both of you.

COLIN. No problem.

JACKIE. You should be ashamed of yourself, leaving an old woman in a place like that.

INNES. It's what she wanted. Have we all a drink? Good. To Colin.

ALL. To Colin.

COLIN. Why?

MAC. You finished them.

COLIN. So I did.

MAC. Too busy burying people to stop and actually think about what you've actually done.

JACKIE. There's no way I'd go through that another two hundred and eighty-three times. Well done.

COLIN. It's just a list. A stupid game.

INNES. It's a list of some antiquity now. It gives a structure to things, but yes – I'm sure there are those who treat it just as a milestone or whatever, and take away nothing from the land. Not you. It's been good for you.

COLIN. To Sir Hugh Munro, then.

MAC. The old bugger.

INNES. Talking about old buggers, Ayrshire beckons.

MAC. Let's go. (INNES *puts on his macintosh.* MAC *lowers his rucksack down and exits.*) Come on, old man.

JACKIE (*still drinking*). Christ. Do you call that a drink? (*She goes to exit. Halfway through the hatch:*) There was one moment.

HELEN. Go on.

JACKIE. No . . . it doesn't matter. (*She exits.*)

HELEN (*pokes the fire, covering up the thumb, and puts the grate over it*). We should have let it go out really.

COLIN. You had to keep him warm.

HELEN. Yes. Goodbye Colin.

COLIN. I found the photograph. (*He takes a rock out of his pocket with a cellophane bag attached to it.*) Do you . . .

HELEN. What?

COLIN. Nothing.

> HELEN *exits.* COLIN *is alone. He detaches the photograph and puts it in his pocket before picking up his bag and beginning to descend. He stops, comes up again and collects the two bags of rubbish before descending and shutting the trap door behind him.*
>
> *They exit.*
>
> *The End.*

A Nick Hern Book

The Nest first published in Great Britain as a paperback original
in 2004 by Nick Hern Books Limited, 14 Larden Road,
London W3 7ST in association with the Traverse Theatre, Edinburgh

The Nest copyright © 2004 Alan Wilkins

Alan Wilkins has asserted his right to be identified
as the author of this work

Cover image: Euan Myles

Typeset by Country Setting, Kingsdown, Kent CT14 8ES
Printed and bound in Great Britain by Cox and Wyman Limited,
Reading, Berks

A CIP catalogue record for this book is available from
the British Library

ISBN 1 85459 817 1